Málaga Travel Highlights

Best Attractions & Experiences

Charlie Wall

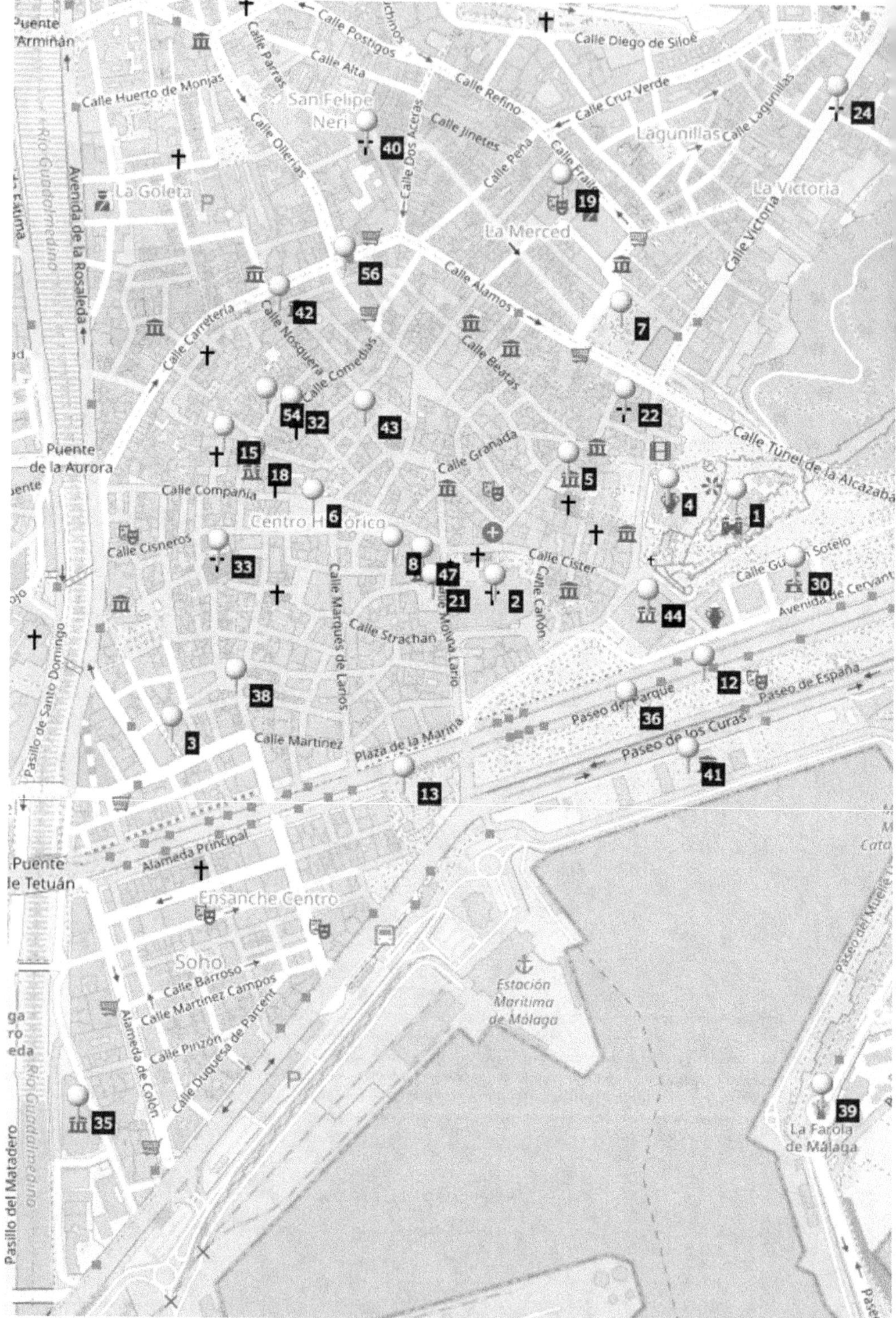

Puente Armiñán
Calle Huerto de Monjas
Calle Parras
Calle Alta
Calle Postigos
Calle Refino
Calle Diego de Siloé
Calle Cruz Verde
Calle Lagunillas
Lagunillas
Calle Lagunillas
24
San Felipe Neri
Calle Ollerías
Calle Dos Aceras
Calle Jinetes
Calle Peña
Calle Fraile
La Victoria
Calle Victoria
La Goleta
40
19
La Merced
P
Avenida de la Rosaleda
Calle Álamos
56
Calle Carretería
42
Calle Nosquera
Calle Comedias
Calle Beatas
7
54 32
43
Calle Granada
22
15
18
Calle Compañía
Calle Cister
5
Puente de la Aurora
Centro Histórico
6
Calle Túnel de la Alcazaba
4
1
Calle Cisneros
8
30
33
47
44
Calle Guillén Sotelo
21
2
Avenida de Cervantes
Calle Marqués de Larios
Calle Strachan
Calle Molina Lario
Calle Cañón
38
12
3
Paseo del Parque
Paseo de España
Calle Martínez
36
Plaza de la Marina
Paseo de los Curas
13
41
Puente de Tetuán
Alameda Principal
Ensanche Centro
Soho
Calle Bárroso
Calle Martínez Campos
Estación Marítima de Málaga
Calle Pinzón
Calle Duquesa de Parcent
Alameda de Colón
P
Río Guadalmedina
Pasillo del Matadero
35
39
La Farola de Málaga
Paseo del Muelle

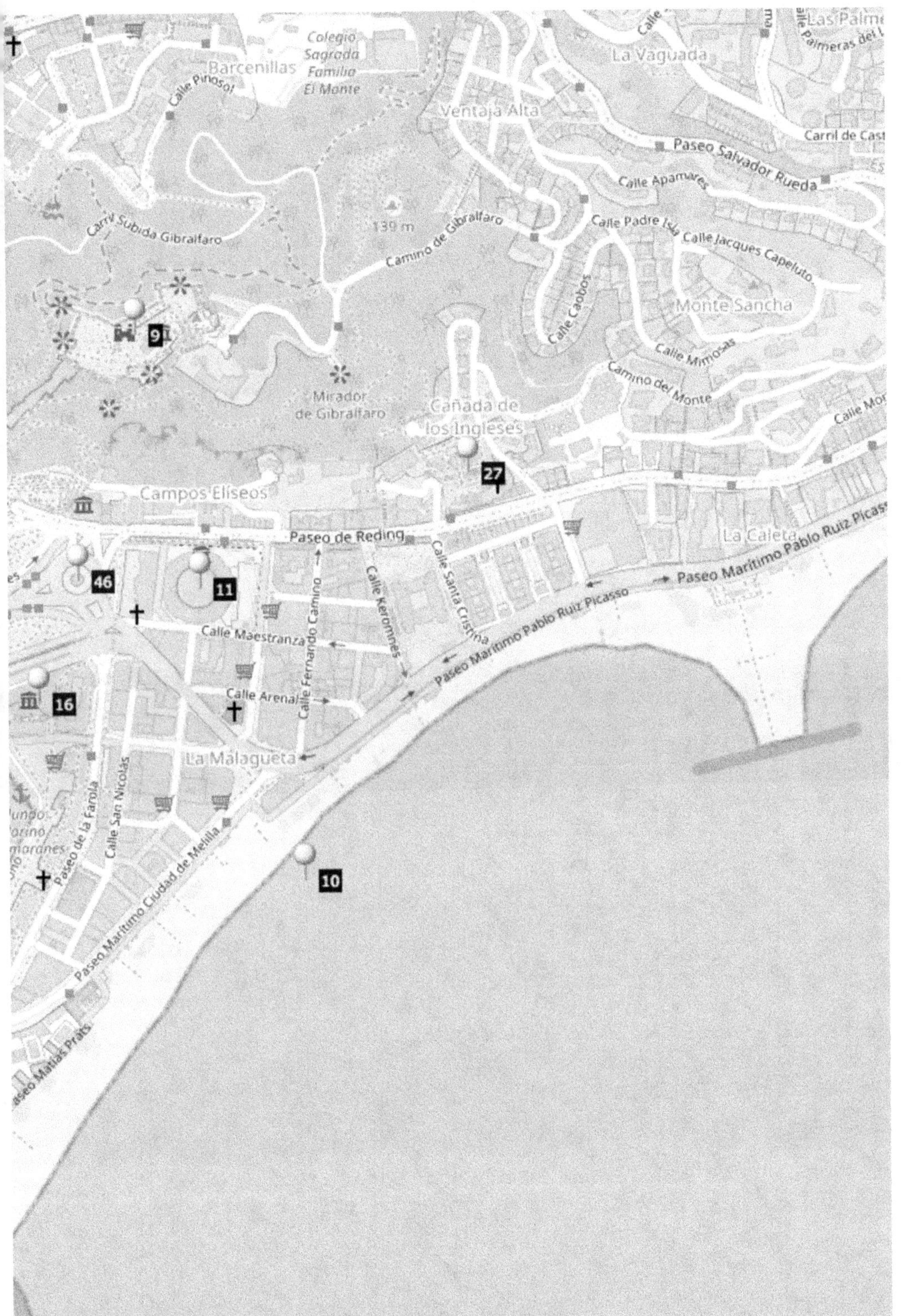

Barcenillas
Colegio Sagrada Familia El Monte
La Vaguada
Calle
Las Palm
Palmeras del
Calle Pinosol
Ventaja Alta
Paseo Salvador Rueda
Carril de Cast
Calle Apamares
Carril Subida Gibralfaro
Camino de Gibralfaro
Calle Padre Isla
Calle Jacques Capeluto
139 m
Calle Caobos
Monte Sancha
9
Calle Mimosas
Camino del Monte
Mirador de Gibralfaro
Cañada de los Ingleses
Calle Mo
27
Campos Elíseos
La Caleta
Paseo de Reding
Calle Santa Cristina
Paseo Marítimo Pablo Ruiz Picasso
46
Calle Fernando Camino
Calle Keromnes
11
Paseo Marítimo Pablo Ruiz Picasso
Calle Maestranza
16
Calle Arenal
Calle Fernando Camino
La Malagueta
Calle San Nicolás
Paseo de la Farola
undo
arino
marañes
Paseo Marítimo Ciudad de Melilla
10
Paseo Matías Prats

Contents

Welcome to Málaga

Málaga, the birthplace of artist Pablo Picasso, is a coastal city on the Costa del Sol in Andalusia in southern Spain. Picasso left in 1895, but his modernist paintings and sculptures have influenced Málaga's art schools and architecture. The city has two well-preserved Islamic citadels, remnants of the era when Spain was part of the Moorish realm. Sunbathers and swimmers frolic in its beaches and in the warm sea while golfers tee off at its world-class courses.

☐ 1. Medieval Castle (Alcazaba)

Address: Calle Alcazabilla, 2, 29012 Málaga, Spain
Phone: +34952227230
Email: sescalona@malaga.eu

Built in the 11th century by Muslim warrior settlers, the imposing fortification of this medieval castle towers over the city of Málaga. It is situated on a high hill above the city with views across coastal plains to Gibraltar and to Africa. The fortification has withstood sieges by both Moors and Christians during its long history. The medieval castle (Alcazaba) was once connected by a walled pathway to the higher Castle of Gibralfaro.

☐ 2. Cathedral of Málaga

Address: Calle Molina Lario s/n, 29015 Malaga, Spain
Phone: +34952220345
Email: catedral@diocesismalaga.es

Built between 1528 and 1782, the Cathedral of Málaga is a perfect blend of Renaissance and Baroque that redefines the architectural magnificence of this southwestern Spanish city. With its intricate stained-glass windows, gold-plated altar, and splendid works of art displayed inside the building, this magnificent cathedral sets aside an awestruck feeling for visitors who are lucky enough to discover the beauty of its bold architectural splendor.

☐ 3. Atarazanas Market

Address: Calle Atarazanas, 10 , 29005 Málaga

Phone: +34 951 92 60 20

Email: info@malagaturismo.com

The Atarazanas Market is the oldest historical-architectural building in Malaga, a beautiful landmark where you can enjoy a tasty plate of food while taking in the culture. The place is a 16th century building that was well restored. It occupies 3,300 square meters and houses local markets, with shops, cafes, restaurants and live music bars.

□ 4. Roman Theatre

Address: Calle de la Alcazabilla, 6-8, 29015 Malaga, Spain

Phone: +34 951501115

The building of the Roman theatre of Málaga began in 19 BC and by 15 BC was already in operation. After the fall of Roman Málaga in 410 AD the Arabs used its blocks to build Alcazaba Castle nearby. The theatre is one of the most important Roman remains in Europe. It is located at the end of Calle Manuel Doblado at the entrance to the Alcazaba Castle. The theatre has three doorways, vestibules with capacity for 15,000 people and the remains of 20 columns.

□ 5. Picasso Museum

Address: Calle San Agustín, 8, 29015 Malaga, Spain
Phone: +34 902 44 33 77
Email: info@museopicassomalaga.org
Web: http://www.museopicassomalaga.org/en/home

The Museo Picasso was first opened in 2003 in the Buenavista Palace, in the city where the artist was born in 1881. The collection is made up of 285 works donated by members of Picasso's family. The museum is based at the former residence of the Ruiz y Picasso family, who were art collectors and amateur painters. During Ferdinand VII's reign, Buenavista Palace was built as a summer residence for them and would later be home to Pablo Ruiz Picasso and then his granddaughters Cristina, Victoria and Marina.

□ 6. Constitution Square

Address: Plaza de la Constitución, 1 , 29005 Málaga, Spain

The Plaza de la Constitución is Málaga's central plaza. Located 10 minutes on foot from the city port, this plaza shows off its elegant style with marble structures and columns. The Plaza was designed in the Spanish Colonial Revival architectural style, built according to the plans of architects Villanueva y Sainz de Ancosa and Rafael Blasco Ferrer Bosch. This historic plaza is situated near many landmarks including Casa de la Poncelle, Palacio Barolo, Plazuela de los Patos, and Palacio de Quevedo.

☐ 7. Merced Square

Address: Plaza de la Merced, 25 , 29012 Málaga, Spain

The Plaza de la Merced is a central plaza located in the barrio La Merced located directly behind the Cathedral of Málaga. It is one of the largest public squares in the city, and includes some of its most iconic attractions. One of these is Pablo Picasso's childhood home which he lived in from 1891 to 1895. Additionally it includes a parish church, a hospital, and a number of historical buildings. Two large fountains can be found on either side of the plaza, and four smaller fountains decorate the center.

☐ 8. Historical Core of Malaga

Address: 3 Calle Fresca, Málaga 29015, Spain

Take a stroll around the historical core of Málaga and marvel at its distinctive Mediterranean architecture. From monumental buildings to its intimate narrow streets, take a break in one of the squares while enjoying a fresh juice, typical coffee, tapas or a cigar.

☐ 9. Gibralfaro Castle

Address: Camino de Gibralfaro, 11, 29016 Malaga, Spain
Phone: +34952122020

For nearly 900 years Gibralfaro Castle has stood watch over the Strait of Gibraltar. The Moorish defensive walls are well preserved, offering great views of Málaga below. Walk the hillside garden to the top of the castle for panoramic views of the city, harbor, and coast. The Gibralfaro fortress is impressive on any day, but sunrise or sunset are the perfect times to enjoy its magnificent views of the city below. The medieval castle (Alcazaba) was once connected by a walled pathway to the higher Castle of Gibralfaro.

☐ 10. Malagueta Beach

Phone: +34 952 224 367

The Malagueta beach is an expansive 2 kilometers of sandy coast located five minutes away from the center of Málaga. For more than 100 years it has been one of the most popular beaches in the city, today it is one of the largest, offering an amazing services range corresponding to all tastes. The sea floor slopes gradually and there is a shallow area frequented by families and kite surfers.

☐ 11. La Malagueta Bullring & Museum

Address: Paseo de Reding, 8, 29016 Malaga, Spain
Phone: +34 952222172
Email: info@la-malagueta.es

La Malagueta bullring is a great place to witness the art and history of bullfighting. The associated museum has a large collection of engravings, lithos and photographs from the second half of the 19th century. Located alongside the Paseo de Reding, this bullring has been a landmark of the city since 1876.

☐ 12. Parque de Málaga

Address: 2 Paseo del Parque, Málaga 29016, Spain

The Parque de Málaga is a beautiful park and is the largest (33 hectares) and most popular in the city and has several water features, gardens and views of the Mediterranean sea and mountains in the background.

☐ 13. Marina

Address: Plaza de la Marina, 11 , 29001 Málaga, Spain
Phone: +34 951 92 60 20

The world famous Marina is both a promenade and a park, which has been built next to the port and has won the interest of tourists and residents for more than 30 years. Many buildings and monuments can be found along the Marina: it is a unique place that marries the history and culture of Málaga to modern urban life and entertainment. Here you can take a meal in one of the restaurants; swim in one of the swimming pools; walk around looking at the shops; or simply sit down on one of the benches and admire the waterfront and the multi-million-Euro vessels.

□ 14. La Concepcion Historical-Botanical Gardens

Phone: +34 951 92 61 79
Email: botanicolaconcepcion@malaga.eu
Web: http://laconcepcion.malaga.eu/

The La Concepcion Historical-Botanical Gardens were founded by Carmelite monks around 1580. They contain some remaining buildings of the convent which was destroyed during the Napoleonic invasion, included the cloister, refectory and part of the church (all 17th century). The first collections were mostly medicinal herbs grown in the monastery's own garden. These collections were distributed to other botanical gardens in Madrid, Barcelona, Zaragoza, Seville and Valencia. A second historical feature are the remains of a Genoese fortification.

□ 15. Temple of the Sacred Heart

Address: Calle de Liborio García, 3, 29005 Málaga, Spain
Phone: +34 952 21 25 81

The Temple of the Sacred Heart is a neo-Gothic church built in the 15 century, located in the Plaza de la Encarnación. The cross of the temple serves as a landmark for those that come from far away to worship from afar. It joins two very different structures, together they make the perfect corner of the plaza. Come here for a mass if you have enough time.

☐ 16. Centre Pompidou Málaga

Phone: +34 951926200

The Centre Pompidou Málaga opened in 1996 in the Andalusian capital. The Centre Pompidou is an art museum that houses one of the greatest collections of modern and contemporary art by Spanish artists in Andalusia. Featuring works by Spanish avant-garde painters such as Salvador Dalí, Joan Miró, Antoni Tàpies and Pablo Picasso, an impressive permanent collection of works is displayed.

☐ 17. Basilica of Santa Maria de la Victoria

Email: victoria@diocesismalaga.es
Web: http://www.santamariadelavictoria.com/

The Basilica of Santa Maria de la Victoria is one of the grandest Baroque churches in Spain. It was erected in the 17th century with a richly ornate facade. The church can be seen from across the city and overlooks the ocean. The imposing structure houses a macabre, bone-filled crypt that inspires fear and wonder even today.

☐ 18. Carmen Thyssen Museum

Address: Calle de la Compañía, 10, 29008 Malaga, Spain
Web: https://www.carmenthyssenmalaga.org/

The Carmen Thyssen Museum, Málaga is an art museum with a focus on Spanish 19th-century painting, built around the collection of Carmen Cervera, fifth wife of Baron Hans Heinrich Thyssen-Bornemisza.   The museum she opened in 1992 in Málaga was separated from the main family collection based in Madrid and organized according to Carmen's own preferences. It focuses on Andalusian and Málaga's art history.

☐ 19. Teatro Cervantes

Address: Calle Ramos Marín s/n, 29012 Málaga, Spain

Phone: +34 902 36 02 95

Web: http://www.teatrocervantes.com/

Theater? Opera? Ballet? Or perhaps a Flamenco show! The Teatro Cervantes, part of the Malaga City of Culture and Music program, offers them all. This historic theater (a branch of the National Theater of Spain) is in the heart of Málaga. Ancient in its origins, yet modern in its design, this theater has become one of the most important meeting places for Málaga's artistic community.

☐ 20. The Treasure Cave

Phone: +34 952 40 61 62

Email: cuevadeltesoro@rincondelavictoria.es

The Treasure Cave is a unique cave that's been shaped over millennia by the mixing of seawater and fresh water. Visitor's can explore the cave's unusual rock formations. Look for the original 8th century Arab inscriptions at the entrance to the cave.

☐ 21. Plaza del Obispo

Address: 5 Plaza del Obispo, Málaga 29015, Spain

The Plaza del Obispo is a large plaza that has been the center of the city for over 400 years. The plaza was named after the Archbishop of Málaga, Andrés de Isla, who died in 1517 and was buried at this site. When you visit, enjoy the attractions such as the street performers or just people-watch the shoppers in the open air market.

☐ 22. Church of Santiago

Address: Calle Granada, 78, 29015 Málaga, Spain
Phone: +34 952 21 96 61
Email: parroquiasntiago@gmail.com
Web: http://www.parroquiasantiago.es/

One of the oldest Christian places of worship in southern Spain, this church is also famous for its Gaudí-esque stained glass. Built in the 15th century over the foundations of an earlier structure, it has a neoclassical façade, but its interior is largely baroque.

☐ 23. Mercado Salamanca

Address: 5 Calle Salamanca, Málaga 29013, Spain

Mercado Salamanca in Málaga, is an awe-inspiring public market and is a cornerstone in the city's history, housing an interior courtyard with stalls where artisans sell fresh goods. Constructed in 1929, Mercado Salamanca's architecture simulates an old-world atmosphere, decorated with tiny windows and ornate archways. Wander through its majestic halls, captivated by the aromas of dried chillies, fresh fish, fresh fruit and much more.

☐ 24. Capilla del Agua

Address: Calle Agua 1, 29012 Málaga, Spain

If you're in the Albayzín district in Málaga, visit the unusual Capilla del Agua. A tiny Baroque chapel from the 17th century. The bright yellow watercolor painting on the ceiling is a lovely piece of art.

☐ 25. Customs Palace (Palacio de la Aduana)

Address: 2 Plaza de la Aduana, Málaga 29015, Spain

A magnificent example of Mudejar architecture, the Palacio de la Aduana was built in the 18th century as a customs house. Its excellent location by the seaside has meant that it has played an important role in the city, both economically and historically. Nowadays, the Customs Palace has been fully restored to allow visitors to enjoy its sumptuous Mudejar-style features and stunning views over the coastline of Málaga.

☐ 26. La Misericordia Beach

Address: 11 Paseo Marítimo Antonio Banderas, Málaga 29004, Spain

The La Misericordia Beach is a hidden gem. It's a tranquil place, a public beach that offers a good range of water sport activities and has a small shipyard where boats are repaired. The beach has rocky, volcanic sand. There are good views of the marina and bay of Malaga. The waters here are clear and warm, but deep. There's also a stone jetty from where you can fish. Locals enjoy an walk at the beach before heading home for dinner.

☐ 27. The English Cemetery in Málaga

Address: Avenida Príes 1, 29016 Málaga, Spain

Phone: +34 952 22 35 52

Web: http://www.cementerioinglesmalaga.org/

Established in 1722, the English Cemetery is set on a hillside overlooking the Mediterranean Sea and the city skyline of Málaga. It is a place of tranquility and beauty as well as a historic landmark that has been important in establishing the English community within the region. The cemetery was founded in 1722 by a group of British merchants from Genoa known as Ingleses. In the early years, the cemetery was adjacent to the British consul's house. In 1802, King Carlos IV granted to this cemetery all rights and benefits of other cemeteries located in Málaga, therefore it became a public burial ground for all persons who died in the city. Today, there are more than 3,000 tombs including those of officers and seamen from various countries.

□ 28. Palo Beach

Address: Plaza del Padre Ziganda, Málaga 29017, Spain

Once you get past the harbor, you'll see a sandy beach filled with lots of people - many of them students and young people. You can take a refreshing dip in the Mediterranean Sea off the popular Paloma Beach, which is backed by a promenade filled with terraces and kiosks. This is not an undiscovered gem, but it's still considered one of Málaga's best beaches.

□ 29. Málaga CF Football Stadium, Museum & Tour

Address: Paseo de Martiricos s/n, 29009 Málaga, Spain
Phone: +34 952 10 44 88

Email: museo@malagacf.es
Web: http://www.malagacf.com/es/museo

The Estadio La Rosaleda is a football stadium that holds 29,000 people and has been the home stadium of Málaga CF since 1929. It also hosted the Club Deportivo Málaga for many years until its dissolution in 2011.

□ 30. Ayuntamiento de Málaga (City Hall)

Address: 4 Calle Guillén Sotelo, Málaga 29016, Spain
Phone: +34 952 13 53 48

The Ayuntamiento de Málaga, or City Hall of Málaga, is located in the heart of the city. This historic and ornate building was built between 1557 and 1571. Nobleman Rodrigo Ponce de León founded it with the help of the Italian architect Juan Bautista Maino, who also built the Plaza de la Constitución.

□ 31. Russian Art Collection

Web: https://www.coleccionmuseoruso.es/

The Russian Art Collection of the Museum St. Petersburg is a set of artworks and artifacts from Russian artists and craftsmen from the 19th century to the beginning of the 21st. The Colección del Museo Ruso San Petersburgo Málaga, Málaga is one of the largest collections of Russian art outside of Russia. The museum was founded in 1991 and comprises over 6000 objects, including works of painting, drawing, sculpture and decorative art from Russian artists such as Ritzevich and Bryullov.

☐ 32. The Church of the Holy Martyrs

Address: Plaza Mártires 1, 29008 Málaga, Spain
Phone: +34 952 21 27 24

The Church of the Holy Martyrs in Málaga is a Baroque-style church consecrated to San Telmo and San Herófilo who were stoned to death. The martyrdom was during the Diocletianic Persecution, about 296/297 AD. The Church was built during the XVIII century and occupies the place where two old churches used to exist: dedicated to San Felipe Neri and San Sebastián, respectively. The building is eclectic, with Baroque elements combined with Iberian-Romanesque decorations.

☐ 33. Iglesia (Church) de San Juan

The Iglesia de San Juan is a Baroque church in Málaga. Built from the mid-18th century onward, it is one of Málaga's most important religious buildings. Designed by the royal architect Pedro Sánchez Galindo and executed by a team of workmen led by Damián Maestre, its construction was sponsored by King Carlos III. It contains some lavish decorations and sculptures, as well as many artworks brought from Italy.

☐ 34. Málaga Plaza shopping mall

Address: Armengual de la Mota 12, 29007 Málaga, Spain
Phone: +34 952 61 40 40
Email: info@malagaplaza.com
Web: https://www.facebook.com/malagaplaza
Web: http://www.malagaplaza.com/

The Malaga Plaza shopping mall is one of the most popular shopping malls in the city. It has a large selection of shops including fashion, accessories, home decoration and technology. This two-level mall also has a food court, several ATMs and parking spaces.

☐ 35. Contemporary Art Museum

Address: Calle de Alemania, s/n, 29001 Malaga, Spain
Phone: +34 952120055
Email: cacmalaga@cacmalaga.org
Web: http://cacmalaga.eu/

The Contemporary Art Museum of Málaga is one of the most important contemporary art museums in the country. Opened in 1999, this fascinating museum is housed in a former market building. It exhibits both new and venerable contemporary artists. The collections are divided into two floors, with a temporary exhibit hall on the top level, complete with several multi-purpose rooms that are used for various cultural events including concerts, lectures, workshops, courses and audiovisual projection. A marble-covered patio with tables and chairs offers an excellent setting for drinks, meals and meetings.

42

□ 36. Monument of Fiestero (Wine Growers)

Address: 2 Paseo del Parque, Málaga 29015, Spain

The monument commemorates the Malaguean wine growers and their Fiesta of El Fiestero, which takes place annually on 14 June. Some years ago, the wine growers used to carry a character called 'El Fiestero' on their procession. This monument was created by Manuel del Busto and was inaugurated in 1982. It consists of a big wine barrel and a sculpture of a group of peasants holding bottles of wine and different objects related to agriculture and wine-growing. The barrel is hollow so there is an interior with glass windows where you can see more sculptures representing the main characters.

☐ 37. Classic Car Museum

Phone: +34 951137001

Web: https://www.museoautomovilmalaga.com/

The Museo Automovilístico de Málaga houses a growing collection of classic and rare cars and motorbikes which spans the history of road and racecar development over the past 100 years. The museum collection includes automobiles, motorbikes and bicycles as well as other items such as advertising material, tools and spare parts. The museum centerpiece is a 1929 Hispano-Suiza H6C Cabriolet.

☐ 38. Plaza de Félix Saenz

Address: 3 Plaza de Félix Sáenz, Málaga 29005, Spain

Famous for its 40x100-meter, Mediterranean-town-style design, the Plaza de Félix Saenz features fountains, decorative sculptures, and lots of space for lounging, eating lunch or having a picnic. Popular among locals and tourists alike, this plaza is also home to Málaga's Museum of Contemporary Art.

☐ 39. La Farola de Málaga (Lighthouse)

Address: 1 Glorieta Joaquín María Pery, 29016, Spain

La Farola de Málaga, Málaga is one of several seaside lighthouses on the Costa del Sol along the Mediterranean Sea.

☐ 40. San Felipe Neri Church

Address: 21 Calle Gaona, Málaga 29012, Spain

The church's interior hides many wonders. San Felipe Neri is a Neo-Classical church with an interior designed by Augustinian architect Aníbal González. It has a single nave with four stalls, each for a different saint. The works were done by great artists - Juan de Mesa, Ventura Rodríguez, Francisco Bayeu y Subías, Francisco Gascué… the list goes on. These are not just artworks in the classical sense but pieces to be admired at close range that reveal their full beauty when you look at them in detail.

☐ 41. Palmeral de las Sorpresas (Palm Grove of Surprises)

The Palmeral de las Sorpresas (Palm Grove of Surprises) is a nice promenade by the port area. You can walk through the Palm Grove on your way to the local beaches.

☐ 42. Holy Week Museum

Address: Calle Muro de San Julián 2, 29008 Málaga, Spain
Phone: +34 952 21 04 00
Email: museoss@agrupaciondecofradias.es

Web: http://www.agrupaciondecofradias.es/

The Holy Week Museum is dedicated to one of Spain's most unique religious traditions, which highlights the lives of popular saints in the Andalusia region.   The museum is a place to contemplate more than 300 religious objects and prints of more than 300 years old concerning the Holy Week ('Semana Santa' in Spanish) processions that are held in the city.

□ 43. Sala Gold

Address: Calle Luis de Velázquez 5, 29008 Málaga, Spain
Phone: +34 670 09 87 49
Web: https://www.facebook.com/SalaGold/
Web: http://discotecasenmalaga.es/gold/inicio/

Sala Gold is Málaga's largest disco club, located in the heart of the city. This place gets crowded every night, especially on the weekends when local people go to have a drink with friends before heading out to party. With professional dancers, excellent lighting effects, and great music, this is one of the top places in the city to have fun.

☐ 44. Museum of Málaga

Address: 2 Plaza de la Aduana, Málaga 29015, Spain

The Museo de Málaga features a fine collection of 19th century paintings and a selection of works from other periods. The Fine Arts Collection includes a noteworthy collection of textiles, as well as other types of items such as furniture and ceramics. Among the most notable works are by the Spanish painters Joaquín Sorolla, Claudio Coello, Mariano Fortuny and Francisco Zurbarán, as well as those from France, Italy and Russia. In addition, there are many pieces made by local artists working at the start of the 20th century.

□ 45. Frigiliana Museum of Archaeology

Address: 4 Calle de la Cuesta del Apero, 29788, Spain
Phone: +34 952 53 42 61
Web: http://www.museodefrigiliana.org/

The museum is located in the Archaeological site of Frigiliana, site of an ancient Iberian town. Visitors can explore two large spaces—the Entrance Hall and the Archaeological Gallery—that together trace Frigiliana's history through its development, starting with prehistoric artifacts displaying the area's earliest inhabitants and other archaeological sites to show the gradual development of civilisation. A large body of work called "Frigiliana in deep time" portrays the timeline of its existence in three dimensions using pieces recovered from excavations around the city.

□ 46. Fountain of the Three Graces

Address: 6 Paseo del Parque, Málaga 29016, Spain

The Fountain of the Three Graces ia also known as the Fuente de las Tres Gracias. The fountain is part of Málaga's historic center and was built around the year 1750 by Carlos III of Spain. Three of the four decorative water outlets are graced by figurines of women who represent beauty, generosity, and bounty.

☐ 47. Palacio Episcopal Málaga Centro de Arte

Open your mind to a world of art and architecture at the Palacio Episcopal Málaga Centro de Arte in Málaga. This popular art gallery features rotating exhibits and is housed in a Renaissance style palace near the cathedral and city hall of Málaga.

☐ 48. Bodega Antigua Casa de Guardia (Wine Tasting)

Address: Ctra. Olías – Comares, s/n, Finca El Romerillo, 29197 Barriada de Olías, Spain
Phone: +34 952 03 07 14
Email: info@casadeguardia.com
Web: http://www.casadeguardia.com/

Known for its spectacular setting, the Bodega Antigua (Old Wine Storehouse) is an original sherry bar dating back to the 14th century and situated near to Malaga's historic city walls. The wine and sherry cellar was built by the Catholic Monarchs and was once a military fortress. The sherry and wine tasting takes place in the underground cellar. The bar ranks among the oldest and most popular in the city. Casa de la Antigua Guardia is an authentic old tavern with exposed stone walls, antique furniture à la française and sherry served by the jug. Admire the ceilings by artist Jerónimo Suñol Mauriño from 1866. Come here to watch Barcelona's match against Malaga CF or indeed any Spanish La Liga football match on TV.

☐ 49. Rio Chillar Walk

Rio Chillar Walk - Málaga - Malaga, Spain The Rio Chillar Walk is located near Berja in Málaga. The walk lasts approximately 1.5 hours and is rated as easy. It starts off along the road before heading into the forest along the Rio Chillar River. The route ends at a waterfall with rocks to jump off, giving you lots of opportunities to cool off on a hot day.

☐ 50. Aquaduct of San Telmo

The Aquaduct of San Telmo is a Roman aqueduct built to bring water from the Sierra Bermeja to the neighborhood of Mariana in Málaga. Generally regarded as the most famous work of architecture built in Andalusia during the period of Arab rule, its construction was between 1172 and 1202 AD.

☐ 51. Palacio de Deportes José María Martín Carpena

The Palacio de Deportes José María Martín Carpena is an indoor sporting and events arena. The arena is the home venue of the Málaga Club de Baloncesto basketball team, and has also hosted major concerts from artists including David Guetta, Bruce Springsteen & The E Street Band, Katy Perry, Christina Aguilera and Rihanna. Built by José María Martín Carpena in 1982, the arena also hosted the European Athletic Championships in 1994 that hosted 47 countries.

□ 52. Picasso Gardens

Address: 45 Avenida de la Aurora, Málaga 29002, Spain

The Jardines de Picasso (Picasso Gardens), show off some of the most beautiful Mediterranean groves and are included in the National Register of Gardens. These gardens are an good place to enjoy nature as well as various artworks from Picasso and other great artists.

□ 53. La Caleta Beach

La Caleta Beach is located between the cliffs of Europe's most filmed coastline of the Costa del Sol. La Caleta Beach has been visited by film stars including Brad Pitt over its illustrious history.

□ 54. Hammam Al Andalus (Spa)

Address: Plaza Mártires 5, 29008 Málaga, Spain
Phone: +34 952 21 50 18
Web: https://www.facebook.com/HammamAlAndalus
Web: http://malaga.hammamalandalus.com/

The Hammam Al Andalus Malaga offers a traditional bathing experience in a beautiful Moorish complex. Take a leisurely dip in a warm outdoor pool or enjoy a variety of treatments, saunas and relaxing areas. The complex has been renovated respecting the original styles, with splashes of pinks, ochres and greens against the classic white walls and dark woodwork - making it as exotic as ever!

☐ 55. La Maroma

La Maroma is located in the Sierras of Tejeda, Almijara and Alhama in Málaga. It is the highest peak of the mountains in this range. The ascent takes approximately 2-3 hours depending on physical fitness, which varies according to the path taken. La Maroma has a height of 2069 meters above sea level. There are different paths to reach it. If you want to try one of them, it is advisable to train beforehand to get accustomed to the altitude.

☐ 56. ZZ Pub & Live Music Venue

Address: Calle Tejón y Rodríguez 6, 29008 Málaga, Spain
Phone: +34 952 44 15 95
Web: https://www.facebook.com/zzpub
Web: http://www.zzpub.es/

The ZZ Pub is one of the city's most popular live music venues. With five bars, two concerts halls with capacity for 2,500 people and three outdoor bars, this buzzing venue offers year-round entertainment. The stage has hosted some of Spain's biggest bands including Extremoduro, Dvicio and Manolo Garcia.

☐ 57. Aqua Velis Water Park

Address: Calle Ruta del Moscatel, 22, 29700 Vélez-Málaga, Spain
Phone: +34 952 54 27 58
Email: info@aquavelis.com
Web: http://www.aquavelis.es/index_en.htm

The Aquavelis water park of Málaga offers more than twenty rides. Its spectacular design is set to impress the most demanding visitors. The Caribbean Beach has five deluxe pools including whirlpools and Jacuzzis, an adults only pool with its own bar terrace and the Cristal Pool, the first infinity pool on Malaga coast which also contains several Jacuzzis, two heart-shaped bubbling beds and there are sun decks available for both adults and children.

Picture Credits

Málaga, Spain Cover: manolofranco / 3745864 (Pixabay)
Cathedral of Málaga: Simononly (CC BY 2.0)
Atarazanas Market: Bikeventures-Manu (CC BY 3.0)
Roman Theatre: Américo Toledano (CC BY-SA 3.0 es)
Picasso Museum: Llecco (CC BY-SA 3.0)
Constitution Square: Simon (CC BY 2.0)
Merced Square: Dguendel (CC BY 3.0)
Gibralfaro Castle: Olaf Tausch (CC BY 3.0)
Malagueta Beach: Elfeffe (CC BY 2.0)
La Malagueta Bullring & Museum: Mer De Glace (CC BY 2.0)
Parque de Málaga: Hedwig Storch (CC BY-SA 3.0)
Marina: Bogdan Migulski (CC BY 2.0)
La Concepcion Historical-Botanical Gardens: Daniel Capilla (CC